Fa

C00022E219

Father's Hands

Paul Cookson

solway

Copyright © 1998 Paul Cookson

First published in 1998 by Solway

04 03 02 01 00 99 98   7 6 5 4 3 2 1

Solway is an imprint of Paternoster Publishing,
P.O. Box 300, Carlisle, Cumbria, CA3 0QS, UK
http://www.paternoster-publishing.com

The right of Paul Cookson to be identified as the Author of this Work has been
asserted by him in accordance with Copyright, Designs and Patents Act 1988.

British Library Cataloguing in Publication Data
A catalogue record for this book is available from the British Library.

ISBN 1-900507-75-7

Some of these poems have appeared in previous collections, published by A Twist in the Tale:
You Took the Words Out of my Mouth (1980), A Twist in the Tale (1981), Waiting for
the Zap! (1984), More Than a Badge (1986), Unclench the Fists (1989), Over 21 and Still
into Noddy (1991), Happy as a Pig in Muck (1991), The Toilet Seat Has Teeth! (1992),
Spill the Beans (1993), Let No-one Steal Your Dreams (1994).

Cover Design by David Parkin
Typeset by WestKey Ltd., Falmouth, Cornwall
Printed in Great Britain by Guernsey Press Ltd

These poems are dedicated
to Mum, Dad,
Sally, Sam, Stuart and Julie

Father's Hands
Contents

Figuratively Speaking

If I speak in pictures
then your ears must be my canvas
and my tongue a brush that paints the words
I want you to imagine.

I'm the James Dean of the poetry world
not one of those crashing bores
but I die very early at every gig
a rebel without applause.

Once Upon a Time Ago

Once
there was a time
when you could not let go
and neither could I.

But now
I have let go
and as I walk away
I find you scratching my back.

Batman May Have Saved the World but He Never Wrote Good Poetry

Looking back on childhood
I remember how, with youthful vision
I wanted to cast off my infant uniform
of duffle coat and short grey trousers
and attire myself in the essential blue tights, red Y-fronts and cape
so that I might be recognised as a hero,
saving the human race my everyday occupation.

But, looking back,
the blue tights were wrinkled, the cape too big and the Y-fronts baggy.
I never acquired x-ray vision or the taste for spinach.
Instead, I only fastened my duffle coat at the neck,
swung tiny fist in a slow-motioned K - E - R - P - O - W!
and painted myself green a couple of times
until I had grown anonymously out of short trousers.
No front-page revelations of daring escapades.
No earth-shattering stories of the saving of humankind
with only two seconds and a laser-proof medallion to spare
or deadly mortal combat with nasty villains whose goal is
world domination with the aid of android vampire hamsters.
No last-minute miracles and getaways due to the lack of
just happening to have my shark repellent spray handy.

So, I chose to wear my underpants beneath my trousers
and although the world lost a potential super-hero
I found that I was liked and respected;
not needing to fight on top of skyscrapers
or defy death too many times to mention:
only needing to be me and to occasionally write poems
that go something like these.

Stalemate

I could not give you what you needed
because you could not give me what I needed.

I could not wipe away your tears
because you could not make me smile.

I could not erase your problems with a kiss
because your touch did not erase mine.
I could not help you bear your pressure
because my pressure was also great.

A look, the hint of a smile,
the yearning for a true loving touch
kept us silent and expecting
but as we expected
no unexpected surge of compassion surprised us
and we were left wanting, needing.

I could not give you what you needed
because you could not give me what I needed.

I was on my high horse
but your castle was too far out of reach.

Remembrance

This year I had no poppy.
I don't know why
but I had nothing to put in my buttonhole
to remind me of the dying
so that I could live in freedom,
live like this today.
No red poppy to remind me
of the blood that was spilt.
No not even silence,
I didn't even stand to attention
for two minutes to ponder the bravery.

This year I had no poppy
but I do not need a red flower
to remind me that someone died
so that I might have life
and have it more abundantly.
My buttonhole may be empty
but my heart is full because everyday
I remember.

If Our Kisses Were Words

If our kisses were words
then we could write them down
and give them to each other
so that we could read them in times of loneliness
and feel the other's presence near.

However our kisses are kisses
and we can only reflect upon
the beauty of those moments shared.

Waiting for the Zap

I'm waiting for the ZAP!
to hit me full in the face and wake me up.

I'm waiting for the thunderbolt to CRASH!
into my heart and jolt me into action.

I'm waiting for the morning when I awake with a BANG!
and I'm really on FIRE!

but my faith keeps going off phphut
and f i z z l i n g   o u t

Where is He Now?

From an angel who liked light
he worked his way down
to a serpent that liked apples.
And down through the ages he progressed
through various stages of goathood
and guest appearances on the silver screen
until now
hardly anybody takes him seriously at all,
laughing at a horned gentleman
with a tail and three-pronged fork
who wears red thermal underwear.
Which is just what he wants
as ouija boards are passed over the counter
in high-street shops
and heavy-metal priests
dramatise fire, brimstone, death and hell
from their records on display at Woolworths.

Jesus Sat Reading Marx

Jesus sat reading Marx with a smile
and more than a feeling of familiarity.

Jesus pondered the idea of communism
remembering how well it had worked for the twelve and himself.

Jesus agreed with the notion of equal opportunity
and help for those who couldn't help themselves,
remembering his sermon on the mount.

Jesus sat and looked at twentieth-century communism
and was filled with sadness.
The tears ran down his cheeks
as he saw how his ideas
had been mixed up, watered down
turned inside out and right around.
He saw how he had been rejected and discounted
and how the freedom to acknowledge him
had been withdrawn with vengeance and violence.

He saw the failure, the evil and the foolishness of man.
He saw the possibilities that were there
but saw the hate, the coldness and the selfishness
and he cried blood for those locked away.
He saw man's inhumanity to man
and he saw how his love was missing and ignored
and because of this he saw the failure.

And he was angry.
Gentle Jesus meek and mild was angry.
He saw what they had done to him
and what they had done to those who loved him
and gentle Jesus meek and mild was angry.
And gentle Jesus clenched his fist
and looked exactly the same as he did
on the day that he cleansed the temple.

War Without Bloodshed

Peace, love and understanding
are words that roll easily off the tip of the tongue
into an acceptable idealistic cliche
that becomes bland with familiarity.

It is very easy to talk of peace and war
saying that war is definitely wrong
and that we long for peace,
until we realise that peace does not just mean
an absence of wars and guns and bloodshed
but a presence of love, caring, forgiveness
and a general coming to terms with the differences within us.

And if we do not have this presence
then all we will have is the war without the bloodshed
and the peace without the love and understanding
. . . which is not peace at all.

More Than a Badge

If all you know is a slogan
and you try to give it breath,
but you don't wear your heart on your sleeve
but a well-pressed badge instead . . .

If you're seen at all the right meetings
when you're strong with all the rest
but alone your hands are an open apology
instead of the militant fist . . .

If you've got the right haircut and fashion,
the look to go with the views,
but then ignore what others say
because they don't look the same as you . . .

If you've got the right papers and posters,
the records with the relevant words,
but all you do is read and tap your feet
when you're hoping to change the world. . . .

If it's style instead of life-style
your commitment part-time forget it.
It's got to be more than a badge and a book
if you're going to give your views credit.

Action speaks louder than words
and even if mine are barely heard
I'd rather be a glimmer of light or a spark
than a hollow pose that's lost in the dark.
Yes, I'd rather be a glimmer that's straight from the heart
than a hollow pose that's lost in the dark.

The Lord Street Ruffle

The fur-ruffled cat stalks in green-ruffled grass
while hair-ruffled ladies with shop-ruffled bags
pass tear-ruffled children with mud-ruffled knees
on car-ruffled streets with breeze-ruffled trees.
Love-ruffled teenagers with kiss-ruffled mouths
have smile-ruffled faces and hug-ruffled clothes.
It's a sun-ruffled day on a wind-ruffled street
and the rush-ruffled people are rushed off their feet
and the wash-ruffled jeans that hang on the line
are waving goodbye to the cloud-ruffled sky.

Thoughts on a Rainsoaked Beach in June

The majestic silence, a peaceful king.
I pray he'll dry your tears and calm the storm inside your heart.
Summer rain on a gently breathing wind,
the whisper of wet sand beneath the spiralling patterns of my feet.

A bleak and ragged coastline hewn with emotion.
Golden domes adorned by spikey green mohicans.
Broken bottles and jagged plastic scar the patterned sand,
scattered shells and driftwood are left like a thousand unfinished dreams.

The intricacy of crustacean forms holds fascination
for my wondering mind: lifeless eyes, brittle casing
unflexed pinchers, multi-jointed appendages, no longer used
looking for all the world like an airfix model I made when I was young.

The lure of the gently lapping ocean.
The magic pull of the beckoning waves.
Memories of paddling barefoot with Wendy,
sharing ambitions and dreams that may be fulfilled one day.

Memories of picnics and crazy games of cricket
and splashing with the laughing smiling children
who for two weeks every Summer have the time of their lives
laughing and shrieking as Geoffrey gets buried in the sand.

Remembered laughter and magic moments,
momentarily lost in the echoes of a distant bell.
And the majesty of silence is enthralling,
and nothing is forgotten, remaining like holiday snapshots that I'm
flicking through on a rainsoaked beach in June . . .

Just Ask Alexander

When those who say belief in God and Christianity
is just a crutch to lean on and help you easily
I'll say just ask Alexander.

When those who say the church is soft then maybe I'll agree
but don't tar all with that same brush because of what you've seen.
Just ask Alexander.

When those who say religion has caused injustice by its piety
I'll say yes but that is our abuse of what we are called to be.
Just ask Alexander.

If God is dead then what's the threat of a lifeless deity?
Why the need to rob their freedom if it's just a fallacy?
Just tell Alexander.

Tell that to a man inside a cell
who believes in heaven but lives in hell.
Tell that to the man whose body bears
savage beatings, bruises, scars.
Tell that to a man whose hunger strike
for a Bible was a fruitless fight.
Tell that to a man whose only crime
is sharing the love of one crucified.
But never ever ever tell him that it's easy.

Palm Leaves

You laid palm leaves before me
welcoming my every move
but they only served to soften the blow
of your execution of my love.

And not for the first time
the love that was supposed to lie down and die
did not.

Batman Never Comes to Retford

Batman never comes to Retford
not because there is no crime
but with all the trouble in Gotham
he hasn't got the time.

Robin never comes to Retford
not because there is no crime
but with all the trouble in Gotham
he's always helping Batman.

Spiderman never comes to Retford
not because there is no crime
but being used to New York City there's no tall buildings
in Retford to attach his webs to.

The Weekend my House Became an Adventure Playground

The house may be tidy.
The ornaments may be safe.
The ghost from up the chimney is gone
letter box monster no longer frightens
and my neighbours are probably
glad of the peace and quiet.
The patter of tiny feet,
niece and nephew's to be precise,
sounded more like a herd of angry elephants
in steel-rimmed clogs
ridden by hyenas high on laughing gas.
Before breakfast.

Yes, the house may be tidy.
The ornaments may be safe
but those little sparks of infant joy
that energised this room
into a battlezone for Ghostbusters
and a car chase for the Batmobile
have taken home with them
a tiny piece of happiness from us all
but trodden oven chips into my carpet.

Hide and seek with dirty linen baskets
blazing smiles from a fireman's helmet,
puddled slides and a mini marathon
running in new wellington boots.
A rainy funfair day, all rides and cuddly toys
and a little girl with sticky hands in mine
who asked if she could have more cloud to eat.
'Look I've got a brew' she proudly said
pointing to a mark upon her leg.
'Don't you mean a bruise?' asked Daddy
'No I've only got one.'

Yes indeed, the house may be tidy.
The ornaments may be safe
and we may well be able
to visit the bathroom uninterrupted.
The oven chips may be swept up
and breakfast may be civilised.
Silence may be golden
but the laughter of children is priceless.

When. . . .

When tender moments do not coincide
and the right thing is said
but at the wrong time and in the wrong tone of voice.

When emotions go unnoticed
and efforts are overshadowed
by more immediate concerns.

When a touch doesn't touch
but interrupts
awkwardly.

When conversations drift aimlessly
all niceties and humdrum
and words are trip-wires.

When it is clear that although our mouths are open
although our fingers touch
nothing is said or done
and we do not communicate.

When this happens
all I want to do is hold you
gently hold you for as long as it takes
until our minds are free
and we can speak and kiss again.
With feeling.

No Amount of Poetry Substitutes Your Presence

If you were here with me now
I would surely kiss you goodnight.

If you were here with me now
I would surely tell you how much I love you.

If you were here with me now
I would surely hold you tight.

If you were here with me now
this poem would surely be a blank piece of paper
emotionless and empty.

No amount of poetry substitutes your presence.

Archaeology For Lovers

Unearthing dead bare memories
excavating long gone corpses
sharing secret skeletons
from so deep inside
it almost fractures to reveal.

And as our strength and love
are made from blood and life
these ghosts will never haunt
there is and never will be
resurrection for these bones.

Skeletons removed carefully from closets
are laid to rest eternally
in deep fathomless graves
the dirt trampled down and forgotten
and immortality is ours to keep unscathed.

The Timing on God's Watch is Always Perfect

When the time is right
everything will fall neatly into place,
barriers will simply fade away
and the cogs will gently slip together
gliding into peaceful action.

When the time is right
understanding will be perfect if not complete,
assurance will feel like the sunshine
and joy will sing like creation
on that resurrection morning.

When the time is right
love will enter like fire
and fly like an eagle
cleansing the depths
and soaring to the highest peaks.

When the time is right
old things will pass away unnoticed
the past will be unmissed
the future be unmissable
and the present unbelievable.

When the time is right
spirits will be filled
with peace and power celestial
the newness be eternal
and faith will be unshakeable.

And when this time has come
grasp it with both hands and mind
and hold it in your heart
for only you will truly know
for only you can truly wait
for only then are you truly ready
when the time is really truly right.

Don't Take the Christ from Christmas

Wine and whisky, crackers, biscuits, turkey, the odd beer.
Chocolates consumed before and after eight and in between.
Nuts and raisins, puddings, cakes, dates and tangerines.
It's really great to celebrate at Christmas.

Fairy lights and holly, tinsel, misletoe.
Christmas trees and things like these make the house a home
but even these don't appease the silence when alone.
It's really great to decorate at Christmas.

Shopping lists are started when Summer holidays end.
Advertisers market their campaigns to fit the trends
hoping that expensive toys will come up dividends.
It's really great manipulating Christmas.

Christmas time means money time . . . and plenty of it.
The chiming singing bells of cash tills ring in profits,
great for those who have but hell if you've not got it.
Then it's grating celebrating Christmas.

Wine and whisky, crackers, biscuits, turkey, the odd beer.
Chocolates consumed before and after eight and in between.
Nuts and raisins, puddings, cakes, dates and tangerines.
It's really great to put on weight at Christmas.

Expensive lists for ideal gifts and things you'd like to have.
It's take and take, make and fake not what you can give back.
And Santa's not commercial so he'll have to get the sack.
It's great to just accumulate at Christmas.

Being full of Christmas spirit, overflowing with good cheer
means being paralytic and buying lots of beer.
Have this on me, one for the road and two for a good New Year.
It's great to be inebriate at Christmas.

The annual church visit, the token Christmas songs.
The service soothes the conscience but it went on far too long
and any trace of brotherhood will very soon be gone.
It's great to be a hypocrite at Christmas.

Wine and whisky, crackers, biscuits, turkey, the odd beer.
Chocolates consumed before and after eight and in between.
Nuts and raisins, puddings, cakes, dates and tangerines.
It's really great regurgitating Christmas.

You took the Christ from Christmas, so tell me what is left?
You took the Christ from Christmas and gave us something else.
If you want a plastic Christmas that's just what you will get.
Is it so great to denigrate our Christmas?

And while we do just what we may to celebrate our Christmas Day
it would be nice to think of Christ, maybe once, maybe twice
and think about the reason we celebrate this season
instead of everything we waste at Christmas.

You took the Christ from Christmas so tell me what is left?
You took the Christ from Christmas and gave us something else.
If you want a plastic Christmas that's just what you will get.
Please don't take the Christ away from Christmas.

Understanding God a Bit

Understanding God a bit
is like listening to your all-time favourite record
again and again and again.
You can listen to it a thousand times or more
and still hear something fresh
that you haven't quite heard in the same way before.
You can sing the words over and over
and still they take on new meanings.
You can remember the buzz
from the very first time you heard it
and the memories that return.
Once you only knew the chorus
but now you not only know the verses word for word
but are getting to grips with the lead guitar break too.

Where once you didn't know why you liked it,
just that you did,
now you know that it is part of you,
the past, the present and the future
and that each time you hear it
your heart will miss a beat
goosebumps rise upon your arms
and shivers race down your spine
as body, soul and mind connect
for those few perfect minutes.

And so it is that listening to your favourite record
is like understanding God a bit more
each time you play it.

A Glimpse Of Heaven on a Yorkshire Landscape

The clouds parted
like a tear in the thick grey woollen blanket
that wrapped around our small forgotten corner of the world
and a solid shaft of light broke through
connecting earth and sky
that made the green greener
the colours sharper and the air clearer
and just for a moment
it looked for all the world as though
Jesus Christ Himself
was beaming down from heaven
just like Captain Kirk from the Starship Enterprise.

And in a way He was.

If I Could Have My Way

If I could have my way
this poem would have loud guitars
and an instant singalong chorus
that would become anthemic on the terraces.
It would be released
as a seven-inch single only
with an equally good B side and no extended remix.

If I could have my way
this poem would reach number one
in its first week of release
and stay there for quite some time.
It would also reach into your home
give you a melody to sing
and thoughts you may consider.

If I could have my way
this poem would have Noddy Holder
singing The Gospel of Saint John
to the tune of 'Merry Christmas Everybody'
And somewhere in the background
Jesus would plug in his guitar
tap his feet, smile and wait
for everyone to sing the words of his chorus.

Look to the future now
it's only just begun . . .

Father's Hands

Father's hands
large like frying pans
broad as shovel blades
strong as weathered spades.

Father's hands
finger ends ingrained with dirt
permanently stained from work
ignoring pain and scorning hurt.

I once saw him walk boldly up to a swan
that had landed in next door's drive and wouldn't move.
The police were there because swans are a protected species
but didn't do anything, but my dad walked up to it,
picked it up and carried it away. No problem.
Those massive wings that can break a man's bones
were held tight, tight by my father's hands
and I was proud of him that day, really proud.

Father's hands
tough as leather on old boots
firmly grasping nettle shoots
pulling thistles by their roots.

Father's hands
gripping like an iron vice
never numb in snow and ice
nails and screws are pulled and prised.

He once found a kestrel with a broken wing
and kept it in our garage until it was better.
He'd feed it by hand with scraps of meat or dead mice
and you could see where its beak and talons
had taken bits of skin from his finger ends.
It never seemed to hurt him at all, he just smiled
as he let it claw and peck.

Father's hands
lifting bales of hay and straw
calloused, hardened, rough and raw
building, planting, painting . . . more.

Father's hands
hard when tanning my backside
all we needed they supplied
and still my hands will fit inside

Father's hands
large like frying pans
broad as shovel blades
strong as weathered spades.

And still my hands will fit inside
my father's hands.

Mum and Dad Are Mum and Dad

Mum and dad are mum and dad.
Well, they are . . . but in some way they're not.
You see, although they didn't actually
bring me into this world
they did bring me up in this world.

Adopted at birth
mum and dad are mum and dad
and always have been.

Never once have I wanted to go back,
trace the roots and dig up the past.
Never once have I wanted to question
face to face and flesh to flesh
with whoever brought me into this world
and then let me go.

What has been is.
What will be is.
What is is.
And never once have I wanted to change it.

Mum and dad are mum and dad.
Always have been
and always will be.

They chose me
and if I had a choice
I know with all my heart
that I could not have chosen better.

The Football Pitch That Dad Built

Dad made a football pitch in our back garden.
He mowed the grass,
marked it out with creosote
and built the goal posts.
They had real nets.

He painted the posts white
just like on Match of the Day
and sent away to a special company for the nets.

They took ages to arrive
but we still played on the pitch
late on Summer nights
and long on holiday afternoons,
all the kids round our way
bringing boots and trainers
to try and score against my dad.

The goals we scored were okay,
may even have been good,
may occasionally have been brilliant
but they were nothing compared to the goals
they would have been with the real nets.
Following that path of the ball
and seeing the net billow with the shot
would always be more spectacular
and would always be more like Match of the Day.
Plus the fact that we wouldn't have to run
twenty yards to get the ball back afterwards
which always took away the thrill of the goal.

At last they arrived.
Dad unwrapped the parcel
and unravelled the nets.
He stretched them between his vice-like hands
testing their strength and smiled his approval.
Eventually the bright orange nets hung over the posts.

He put the ball down, took three paces back,
ran . . . and then . . . thump!
The ball flew into the top corner.
The net billowed gracefully.
Then broke
and the ball went twenty yards behind the goal.

Often the net broke, even with our shots,
but it was worth spending time
knotting the net together again
just to see that one shot
hit the top left-hand corner
leaving the goalie helpless
just like Goal of the Month
on Match of the Day.

Remembering the Yellow Submarine

'The yellow submarine'
a tree trunk forked
one bough high
one bough low
just above the brook
sometimes flooded, sometimes not
where we used to meet
all those years ago.

The creaking bough beneath our weight,
four or maybe five
swinging swaying singing playing
furry pussy willow tails
tickling our cheeks
as water trickles, drips beneath our feet.

Now I cannot remember
everything we did
or every game we played
in that once-special place
just like I cannot remember
all the words in the song
just the chorus
just the fact it was the 'yellow submarine'.

It may be long, it may be gone,
it may almost be forgotten
but all it takes is just one phrase,
two words of that first pop song I ever heard,
and memories wash over
as the yellow submarine
submerges for adventures once again.

I Just Pretend to Like Horses

I don't really like horses to tell you the truth.
I just pretend to.

If I'm honest I'm a little bit scared of them . . .
I suppose it stems from a particularly fat one
resting its weight on my foot at a garden party years ago
to leave a bruising purple arc across my toes
so I pretend to like them.

I don't really like holding my hand out flat
too close to those rubbery lips and chomping teeth
but I pretend to.

I'm not that keen on scratching their ears
and matted dry and dreadlocked manes
but I pretend to.

I don't like visiting them every day
I don't think that they're fascinating or great
but I pretend to.

It's just that Sam is nearly three and loves them
so we go each Summer night to throw leftover carrots
and cauliflower leaves over the gate,
watch them roll in the dust, legs in the air,
and scratch their necks on fence posts.

Enthralled by their every move
his eyes are bright and enquiring,
his words an awe-filled why why why?
And the laughter . . . just the laughter.

And it is in these moments
that there is no pretending.
In these moments
I really do love those horses.

So Far . . . So So

For eighteen years, half my life
moments have been cultivated into verse.
Chiselled words carved into stone poetry.
Tablets held for all to see.
Tablets to read, reread, dissect, digest or discard.

The trivial and mundane.
The banal and sentimental.
The heartfelt and personal.
The childish and childlike.
The cheap and idle pun.
The fact, the fiction.
The word games and trickery.
The truth and half-truth.
Confessions and proclamations.
All sit side by side by side.

Recorded for posterity, or not.
Given equal billing, a page for each.
The worthy and the unworthy.
All with their own footnote in my history.

For eighteen years, half my life
poems become pamphlets become books.
My moments scattered far and wide
sometimes I'm not so sure whether I've sold my heart
or souled my art.

For eighteen years, half my life, this has been my work
and from this moment on, looking back
this work will have taken more than half my life.

So here we are, another moment shared.
Not so much so far so good as so far . . . so so.

Poetry in progress.
Poetry and progress.
Poetry.
Progress.

All Things Being Equal

When you're a three-year-old boy
the world is a great and exciting place.
New experiences collide and clash
yet fit together side by side
each brand new one equally as important as the last.

No adult discretion discriminates.
No grown-up sensibilities think about
such things as right times and right places.
Reality takes a long back seat
and simple surrealism takes over.

Early Learning animals assume real lives
so that not only can the small plastic cow
give milk to a frog half its size
but it can also fight off the solid rubber gorilla
four times its size and weight
before riding off into the sunset on Thomas the Tank Engine.

Biblical prophecies can be fulfilled and extended
when the lion lies down with the lamb
and Winnie the Pooh, Tigger, Mickey Mouse,
Sooty and Postman Pat and his black and white cat as well.

The bath where ducks swim, carpets are liberally flooded
and where bubbles adorn the room
like scattered clouds and Father Christmas's beard
may well be exciting
but it's not half as fascinating
as looking into the toilet
after a particularly spectacular poo.

Analysing the shape and formations of these specimens
is a hitherto undiscovered art form.
That and counting them.
There will be a moment's pause, a quizzical turn of the lips
then with a triumphant point, the exclamation
'That one looks like a dolphin Daddy!
Look! It's like a dinosaur's tale!'

The contents of the nose and trousers are equally enjoyable,
especially their ability to change shape and size.

Hide and seek means
that as long as the head is covered
and they cannot see you
it must be a really good hiding place
even if it does mean that you can see
a neck, body, arms and legs beneath the tea towel.

Words and language are bent and shaped
then moulded into something new.

'Let's pway Daddy' sound holy
until you realise that it means
'Let's pway football.'

Songs are adapted and changed at will
so that Old MacDonald had a farm
and on that farm he had a . . . burger
as well as some chips and a Coke.

Buzz Lightyear no longer says
'To infinity and beyond'
but 'To infinity and be blonde'
and is subsequently transformed into
an intergalactic hairdresser.

'Daddy, your head is shaped like a squaretangle.'

Yes, all things being equal
this is a magical time where innocence means
that all things are acceptable
but innocence will quickly pass
and very soon that time will come
where breaking wind in front of relatives
is not so cute and funny
regardless of the variation in pitch and resonance.

It Was Not an Argument

It was not an argument.
There were no raised voices
but crossed lines became cross purposes
and at one stage I feared
I would be alone, freezing and exposed,
waiting for my train.

But it was not an argument
and I didn't have to spend
five cramped hours
with a Walkman and a cup of tea,
rereading magazine pages
while contemplating fault lines
and how to rebuild a broken bridge.

Because it was not an argument
I sat looking through a dusty British Rail window
having held you tight and kissed goodbye
without tension.
And you, smiling and holding the hand of our son.
You, almost embarrassed and sheepish
while I made faces from within,
bug eyes, wonky tongues and exaggerated kisses
and Sam, excited by trains,
hat down beneath his ears in the harsh Winter wind
pink-cheeked with a grin that could not be widened
blowing machine-gun kisses
until we faded from each other's view.

And it is because it was not an argument
that these are the pictures I cherish, hold close
and travel with.

Grandad Albert's Funeral

I never called him Grandad Albert.
He was christened that because Sam became confused
Grandad Buss
Grandad Cuckoo
Big Grandad George
and then Grandad Albert.

He was always my Grandad
but he was never the type of Grandad
you read about in fiction.
But then again who is?

On Eastbourne Summer holidays
I would rise early each morning to go and buy his paper
knowing that he would give me pennies for a comic
and eventually The Beano became The New Musical Express.
Those Summers were good but maybe it's too easy
to write while wearing rose-tinted spectacles
because for every moment that glows
there are at least one or two or three
where he could have done more
but didn't.

And here we are, thirty or so,
gathered together one last time for him
knowing that the words we hear about him may be true
but knowing that the truth is much less
than the words we hear about him.

It is something of a soulless affair.
No organ to strike the right chord or help the half of us
as we strain to hit the notes on Psalm 23.

And as the curtain closes
I'm wanting to think something, just something . . .
My memory turns back the pages
to the last time I saw him.

Old, very nearly deaf,
worse than I'd ever seen him,
a shadow of his former beery self
he sat in his room at The Home
and emptied his pockets of the teatime biscuits and apples
he would keep for later but never eat.
He could not understand Sam's words
so I translated and exaggerated the jokes and questions
of a four-year-old great-grandson.
I remember him laughing, really laughing,
red-faced throaty laughter
as Sam threw his monkey puppet from a first-floor window.
I remember that.
That and the one-pound coin he gave him for his piggy bank.

We shook hands, embraced,
said 'See you next time then'
never knowing there wouldn't be a next time
never knowing that was Goodbye.

Sympathy for Judas

A kiss
Thirty pieces of silver
Betrayal
These have cast you as villain for eternity.
Your name – synonymous with all things despicable
Your name – an insult to all things loyal.

You walked with Him
You talked with Him
Lived with Him
Breathed with Him
You must have laughed and joked with Him
Believed in Him
Yet still you did that deed.

What could it have been that drove you to that point?
Greed
Frustration
Ideology
Revolution
A gesture to spark the flame of uprising
A mark of failure and ridicule . . .

In that moment when a kiss became treachery
Your past became forgotten, your name immortal,
Everything you'd ever done blotted out completely
One action in time that set execution wheels in motion.

Universally decried, reviled and despised
You are the man who turned his back on Christ
The man who sold God
The man who sold the world

But if it hadn't have been you
Who would it have been?

We could all have been you
Any one of us could have betrayed our God

Any one of us have betrayed our God
Day by day in the things we choose to do.
Day by day in the things we choose not to do.

Failure and betrayal – humanity personified
Hand in pierced hand with resurrection power
Hand in pierced hand with redemption and salvation.

I am Judas
You are Judas
We are all Iscariot.

Let him who is without sin cast the first stone.

Choices, There Are Always Choices

'Deliver us from evil and lead us not into temptation . . .'

Oft-repeated words, heartfelt words
and when we fall from grace
we claim absolute weakness
in the face of overwhelming temptation
and seek to justify ourselves with half-truths, lame excuses
scurrying like rats caught in a barrel
yet still self-centred vanity's attempting
to deflect the blame and guilt and shame elsewhere.

There are no excuses.
Choices, there are always choices.

Circumstances
The Devil
Selfish human nature

These are no excuses.

Responsibility cannot be absolved
Responsibility cannot be ignored

There are no excuses.
Choices, there are always choices.

And when we are led into temptation
it is because we lead ourselves into that place
and choose that it be so.

There are no excuses.
Choices, there are always choices.

This Is My Son in Whom I Am Well Pleased

The first smile
Those first few faltering steps
The first time you said 'Mummy' and 'Daddy'.

Your first goal at football – left-footed too
The first time you caught a ball.

When you said that you wanted to make the old lady better,
Give all your pennies to poorly children
And protect animals from naughty men.

How good you were at Grandma Buss's funeral
Wanting to squeeze mummy's tears away
While telling her that it's okay, she's with God and Jesus
And we'll see her when we die so that's okay.

Showing the dentist your teeth
Not crying at the doctor's with your injections
Wanting to share your thirteen Easter eggs.

When you understood the stories
Asking logical questions
Writing your name without copying.

First day at school, new uniform and lunch box
First merit mark for trying hard
That swimming lesson when you swam without your armbands.

These are all moments
when I burst with pride and love and joy and think
'This is my son in whom I am well pleased'

Moments when for a split split second
maybe, just maybe, I catch a fleeting glimpse,
a cinematic blur, an imperfect imitation
of God the loving Father.
Of course there are those other moments too
when love, patience and forgiveness are needed.

And perhaps in these moments also
there is more to learn about the Fatherhood of God
and how we too may feel the pleasure and the pain.

Superman on the Toilet

Superman, aged 4½,
sits on the toilet.
His cape hung on the bathroom door
and his tights inside out and crumpled
beneath his dangling feet.

It has been a busy day
saving the world from naughty criminals
in between the Teletubbies and Children's Television.

Aged 4½, Superman has singlehandedly . . .

Saved Teddy from a man-eating crocodile
(ten centimetres long, made in Hong Kong)

Assisted Sweep the glove puppet in fending off
a rubber Tyrannosaurus Rex by throwing him down the stairs,
chipping the wallpaper and paintwork in several places.

Demolished a Lego house all over the dining room floor
after rescuing Woody the Cowboy and little Batman.

Crushed salt and vinegar crisps into the living room carpet.

Stamped on three invading ants in the kitchen.

Caused a tidal wave of blackcurrant juice
to sweep over the table's edge with a mere flick of the wrist.

Made three chocolate biscuits disappear
yet strangely left two half-chewed crusts
on the Thomas the Tank Engine plate
and then smeared jam on his cloak.

Also, he watered the tree in the garden.
All by himself.

Superman, aged 4½,
sits on the toilet,
concentration on his face,
making noises Lois Lane has never heard
and then decides he's tired.

Superman, aged 4½,
even with superhero powers
cannot summon the strength to tidy toys away
and sometimes cries when he has to eat mashed potatoes.

Superman, aged 4½,
mission accomplished, job done,
takes far too much toilet roll
(such is his Kryptonite strength)
but still cannot work the flush system by himself.

It has been a hard day.
Superman cleans his teeth
and kisses us goodnight.

Uncle Bill's Shop

Uncle Bill's shop was an Aladdin's Cave
– as long as Aladdin was interested in
bicycles, hardware, haberdashery, pink paraffin
and occasionally toys.

Darwen, Lancashire.
Gregson's Hardware.
Front room of an end terrace.
Corner of a cobbled street.

Never our real Uncle.
Mum and dad always referred to them as
Uncle Bill and Auntie Nora
he was always Uncle Bill to us.
He'd smile and fiddle with his camera
as Auntie Nora served tea in china cups
carried on a tray which bore images of the Beatles
who I had never heard of.

I don't think they paid much attention to them either
but they did have a toy guitar, from the shop I think,
red and cream, badly drawn faces and signatures
at each rounded corner
that I would strum tunelessly on
before pretending it was a ray gun to shoot my sisters.

His shop – a maze of bits and bobs,
odds and sods and this and that.
I know now that he sold many things
but all I was interested in then were the bikes and the cars.

Bicycles hung from the ceiling
while bells and pumps and puncture repair kits
littered shelf space in their higgledy-piggledy order.
And the cars, the Matchbox cars,
rows and rows of Dinky's, Corgi's and the rest.

Each time he visited us
a box would be magicked from a tweed jacket pocket.
Each time we visited him
we'd have a choice from the display on the counter.
Sometimes, the choice would seem too much
and time would pass as we to'd and fro'd deciding . . .
tractor, trailer, transporter, truck . . .
digger, dragster, beach buggy, sports car or saloon . . .

Once I chose a Lambourghini Marzal in green and white
with opening bonnet and doors and suspension on the wheels.
Back at school when childish chatter turned
to the cars we'd have when we grew up
I waited until Jaguars and Rolls Royces had been mentioned
then bragged I'd have a green and white Lambourghini Marzal,
it being the only sports car I could remember.

Uncle Bill would smile and remove it from its box
and the time would fly with cars negotiating hearth rugs,
hairpin bends round dining chairs
and vertical inclines up the back of the fringed sofa.
The long journey home across the winding hilltops late at night
on the top of Tockholes with the stars glinting above
and the streetlights of distant towns in the valley below
even Blackburn looked like fairy land
as we drifted into dreams,
Matchbox Cars safely gripped in thankful fingers.

Uncle Bill and Auntie Nora are long gone now
but the cars he gave were kept by mum.
Chipped, bent, doorless and tyreless
they have been brought out over the years
and tirelessly played with by visiting families.

Thirty years on, I'm taken back in time
and a generation dissolves as Sam empties the toy box,
takes out the Lambourghini Marzal
and negotiates hairpin bends
around dining room chairs
and the vertical incline of Grandma's sofa.

When the Bullocks Ate the L Plates on My Dad's Grey Ford Cortina

It was Summer in the Seventies and seventies in the shade
I was wearing flares and tank tops and I sung along with Slade
And we holidayed in Wales where the green green grass was greener
When the bullocks ate the L plates on my dad's grey Ford Cortina

A chalet that slept three now slept six in Anglesea
In the middle of a field for my family and me
Where the sea view that we view could not have been serener
When the bullocks ate the L plates on my dad's grey Ford Cortina

From the chalet down the valley we could amble to the sand
But I didn't dilly-dally, rambled faster than I'd planned
Past the creatures with horned features reaching beaches that were cleaner
When the bullocks ate the L plates on my dad's grey Ford Cortina

But the bullocks on our hillock had a mighty appetite
Amazing with their grazing, eating everything in sight
I was scared of the herd that shared our green arena
When the bullocks ate the L plates on my dad's grey Ford Cortina

Overnight they had a bite as they tripped their light fantastic
Scrumping from our bumper strips of string and squares of plastic
Incredible but edible – a bovine vacuum cleaner
When the bullocks ate the L plates on my dad's grey Ford Cortina

So I welched back from those Welsh Black not to beef about the bush
Going faster in the pasture of the grass there I'd bullrush
This toreador was sorrier for not being brave or meaner
When the bullocks ate the L plates on my dad's grey Ford Cortina

Moving with the grace of emphysemic ballerinas
Bellowing the bass notes on broken concertinas
Oxo cubes on legs with brooding misdemeanours
When the bullocks ate the L plates
When the bullocks ate the L plates
When the bullocks ate the L plates on my dad's grey Ford Cortina.

My Hands Were Never Like My Father's

My hands were never like my father's.
Too small, too soft, too weak.
They never really weathered the outdoor storms
of building, planting, painting,
nettle grasping and thistle pulling.
True, they've done those things
but somehow they didn't seem built for that.

These hands have caught chickens,
lifted bales of hay and straw,
tightened ropes (badly),
carried cabin sections,
been stained green from the stems of tomato plants
or black from creosote.

They have done all these things and more,
blistered, chafed and sore.
They have done all these things and more
yet never felt totally at ease,
relaxed, at one, moulded to these tasks
but sometimes clumsy, somehow detached
always keen for the gloves and plasters,
warm water and Swarfega
they seemed to feel the pain
before my father's and my brother's.

Maybe they were indoor hands.
I wanted them to be guitarist's hands
but my fingers were too short for bar chords
and too sluggish to skim along the strings
for the flourishes and flashes I desired.

Instead they've gripped countless pens and pencils,
sketching words and pictures
some good, some bad, some ordinary.
Cartoon forms, poems, songs . . . and more,
these hands of mine
dance to shapes and rhythms in my head.
My hands were never like my father's hands.
Until now.
I, a father, have a father's hands
that can be to my son what my father's were to me.

My father's hands
They too can swallow tiny fists
Push swings, throw balls for bats to hit
Cut cardboard shapes, make puppets live . . .

My father's hands
Draw dinosaurs or Batman masks
Take him swimming at the baths
A thousand household normal tasks . . .

My father's hands
Though not so good at DIY
May build his Lego houses high
Or wipe his tears when he cries . . .

My hands now do the things
my father's did with me.
My hands are now a father's
with responsibility.

And as my hands still fit inside my father's hands
my son is now the same as me, you see.
And as his hands fit inside his father's hands
His father's hands now belong to me.
Father's hands now belong to me.

Through the Eyes of God

I'd like to see through the eyes of God
or wear a pair of his glasses just once.

I wouldn't see the way you appear
the imperfections of our bodies
the blemishes or features that distract
those first impressions on which so often we are judged.
I wouldn't see those human failings
but the way you really are:
the smile within your soul
the kindness in your heart
and the love you have to give.

I would see the formation of the wind
the hands that clap the thunder
and the sunshine at the speed of light.

I would see each snowflake in a blizzard
each grain of sand on every beach
every single one in perfect clarity.

I would see the wings of a hummingbird in slow motion
the growth of the forest in the time it takes to blink
the sheen on the lion's teeth and count the legs on
caterpillars.

Horizons would vanish and limits disappear
no detail too small
no feature too large.

In one second I would see the whole universe
each star, each moon, the inside of the sun
and still have time to count the salt within the sea.

And I could not take this in fully
for my mind is far too small.
Not too small to understand the beauty,
the glorious details of heaven and earth but too small
to understand the greed, the hate, the selfishness,
the suffering, the sorrow and the pain,
the wounds of war, the tears from abuse,
the pious smiles of self-contentment
and the darkness of the human spirit.

And if I did see through the eyes of God
or wore his glasses just once
I would see all of creation and why he said
that 'it is good'
but also why he saw the need
to give this broken world an example of himself.
Perfection became flesh and bone
and Jesus wore those dusty sandals,
prepared himself for nails and thorns
and walked and talked and showed us
how we might overcome
and how we too may see the world
through the eyes of God.

Poetry So Ordinary You Do Not Need a Dictionary

I don't want to write poetry for intellectuals and critics
in carefully constructed coded metaphors.

No flowery language or tortured artist stance
but real everyday words about real everyday things

I want to write poetry that captures the here and now
and celebrates that fleeting moment.

Poetry that puts its finger on
exactly what you're feeling this very minute.

Poetry that hits the nail on the head
and then moves on or is forgotten.

Poetry that tells you jokes and trivia
and makes you laugh, cry or just remember.

Poetry that weaves its way into your mind
for the same length of time you hum the latest number one hit.

Poetry that makes you say
'Yeah . . . I've thought that as well'.

Poetry that uses words like snot, snog and bum
and has no snobbery or embarrassment.

Poetry for everyone, young or old
and especially those not interested in poetry.

Poetry that masquerades as nothing else
than words on a page that you may or may not like.

Poetry so ordinary
that you can understand it without the use of a dictionary.

Poetry that makes you want to remember it
and tell it to a friend.

Poetry that makes you think
that you could write it too . . . and probably write it better.

And if I do just one of these
then maybe, just maybe, the poetry I write
will have been worthwhile.